Some Said We Wouldn't Make It, but God! II

Catherine Judkins Allison

ISBN 979-8-88685-507-4 (paperback)
ISBN 979-8-88685-508-1 (digital)

Christian Faith Publishing
832 Park Avenue
Meadville, PA 16335
www.christianfaithpublishing.com

Printed in the United States of America

Ella and Andrew

One of my sisters has a story to share. She graduated from Virginia State Petersburg. Her friend all during college asked her hand in marriage before leaving for Florida to make their home. Of course, she said yes. They were both teachers when they got to Florida. Only Andrew could find a teaching job. She tried for months to no avail. After trying and much sadness, we talked. And we talked about what she loved to do: help other people. She went back to change her profession and become a registered nurse. She stayed on the job for thirty-five years and spent two years helping seniors get the best health care on paperwork. During this time she mothered two fine children, one son and one daughter.

CHAPTER 2

Their children went to school and then to college. Both received their master's. Andrea received a master's and works as a speech therapist. The other child, Marican, received a master's in business administration and works in the government. Ella has four grandchildren, three boys and one girl. Regina is in the third year of college. Ella works with her helping seniors. She works with the prayer group. Her sorority helps seniors get ready for college. She gets clothes together for charities. She spends time with her family and makes videos for our family reunion. Her time is spent making sure others make it to their best. Family is important to her.

Every child of God can defeat the world, and our faith is what gives us this victory. (1 John 5:4 KJV)

CHAPTER 3

Terrie and Ben

My daughter is married to a fine young man who is a hard worker. They have two children: one girl, Erika, who is a college graduate, and one son, Ben II, who is in college. My daughter has always been a go-getter hard worker. She graduated from high school and decided she wanted to go into the Army. She decided she was going from then. After her Army and reserve duty, she went to college and received her bachelor's in business. She trained a lot and got to know the business. She traveled many countries in the military. Her job required her to travel many cities and states. In doing all this, she never forgot to help the needy and the seniors. She made time for her family and her birth family. Terrie and Ben are very close, and they work together so their life can be successful. Being a blessing to others is one of their mottos.

Jesus grew in wisdom and stature and in favor
with God and men. (Luke 2:52)

Tyhe and Felicia

Tyhe finished high school and entered the military. He served and traveled the world. While there he married a lovely person. Though she got sick, my son loved her and worked with her and loved her even more. Through her sickness, she cared for her parents and worked. She could with the help of God, her husband, and her family. Their love is very real, and they believe in God. They raised a son and trusted God for that. They realized without God, they can do nothing. They love and support family.

I have loved you with an everlasting love.
Therefore, I have drawn you with loving kindness.
(Jeremiah 31:3)

Shadquille

Shadquille is our first grandson from our late son. He is a quiet child like his father until you get to know him. He graduated from high school and then went on to do retail business. He has been promoted to a manager. He is saving his money to promote his dream. He styles hair and clothes, and several of his styles have been used and promoted. His patent will be out soon. He has a great mother and siblings. We pray for him that God covers him and his family.

Be completely humble, be patient bearing with one another in love. (Ephesians 4:2)

CHAPTER 6

Gary L. II

He has grown into a fine young man. He was on the National Honor Society all through high school. He played football and soccer. He graduated from NCCU in 2019. After 2019, he received a full ride to North Carolina State University for his master's degree. He graduated in 2021. While in college he started a business, helping school children with their grants and scholarships. He spends time with the parents, showing how to best prepare for college. He believes in education and does his best. He has spent time working in the District Attorney's Office and the States Attorney's Office. In January he starts his last leg for his PHD. Then off he'll go into the work field. His school career has been a blessing to so many people. Some said he wouldn't make it, but God.

"For I know the plans I have for you," declares the Lord, "plans to prosper you and not to harm you, plans to give you hope and a future." (Jeremiah 29:11)

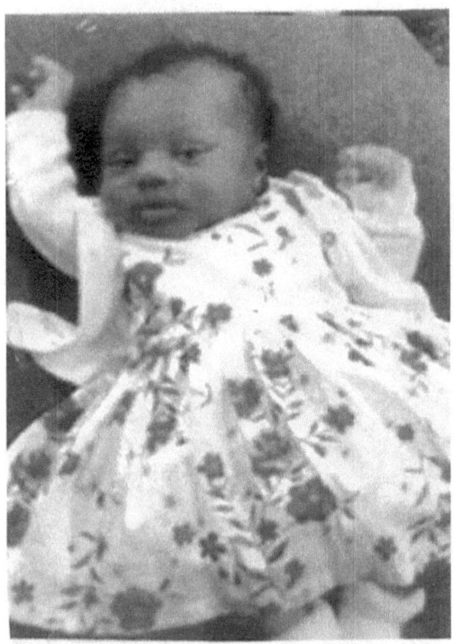

Gianni

CHAPTER 7

Stuart (Trey)

This young man started out to be a social worker and changed his major. He wanted to help people but be able to work with his hands. He graduated from Lincoln Tech with a degree. He has worked in Dallas and now works in North Carolina. He wanted to travel and see different places, and he is doing just that. In school he played football and shined in the last game. When the TV in the kitchen wasn't working, he used the George Foreman grill cord and hooked it in the back of the TV. It started working again. Everybody asked, "What made you do that?" Next, when the car wouldn't start, he put hand sanitizer on the car key, and it started. He loves to debate. He loves people and family. His life has just started. He believes in prayers and helping others.

A Friend Loves at All Times. (Proverbs 17:17)

CHAPTER 8

Ben

Ben is the last to become an HVAC technician. Then he will be going to work in the field. He is going to own his own business. He always wanted to own his own business. He has traveled to many countries and states with his parents. He loves his family and shows it. He is very independent.

With God All Things Are Possible. (Matthew 19:26)

CHAPTER 9

Lindsay

Lindsay is a dancer. She has received many honors and trophies. She travels to many states to dance. Many churches have her dance whenever they have service. She was promoted to teach the toddlers from two to four years of age. The yearly performance was worth the money for the ticket. Now she is getting ready for her second year of college. She will be teaching the young children. She desires to own a dance studio. Lindsay loves all the people who come to see her dance and Ms. D, Ms. Cynthia, Ms. Linda, Ms. India, Ms. Tyrisa, and her friends—Renee, Leah, Danielle, and Donte.

Jesus Christ is the same yesterday, today and forever. (Hebrews 13:8)

CHAPTER 10

Lisa

Lisa is the third child. She graduated with a 3.50 grade point average. She went to community college and work. She was in retail and banking. She loves the hotel business. Now she has her Bachelor of Arts degree and works as a general manager of a hotel. We are so proud of her because she never gave up. She has three children. Gary, the oldest, just graduated with his master's degree. He will be going for his PHD in January. He works with children getting ready for college, looking into grants and scholarships. Next is Trey. He is an HVAC technician, he is working, and we are proud of him. He is doing a great job living in North Carolina. Lindsay is the last child. She is in her second year of college. She is a dancer and a debater and loves children. She wants to open a dance and etiquette studio upon graduating.

You will eat the fruit of your labors, blessing
and prosperity will be yours. (Psalm 128:2)

CHAPTER 11

Nick

Uncle Nick

Nick is my second child. He has one daughter, Nickolette, who's in middle school, and a son named Delonte. Nick works at Howard University Hospital and is well-liked. He likes helping seniors with obtaining benefits and completing any paperwork they need. He works as a shop steward to help people be treated fair—that's a lot of work. He spends a lot of time with his daughter. He loves sports and fishing. He takes the time to plan vacations to spend time with his daughter. He loves his family.

The Lord has heard my cry for mercy, the Lord accepts my prayers. (Psalm 6:9)

MY MENTORS OF LIFE

Mother Adams, Mother Williams, Mother Mosby

Bishop and First Lady Barley

Bishop and First Lady White

Mother Adams told me not to leave the church. I will always remember this day. I wonder how she knew that was on my mind. I was like a child being born again, and I couldn't understand why we couldn't love everybody. Mother Adams encouraged me to keep loving.

CHAPTER 13

Mother Mosby was a woman of prayer. She told me to keep on caring for others because that's what's in my ministry, to help others. I am so glad I met this wonderful lady.

CHAPTER 14

Bishop Williams always told me to trust God for everything.

> *A gentle answer turns away wrath.* (Proverbs 15:1)

Bishop and First Lady Barley, my pastor and first lady, are my blessed examples. Let nothing stop you from trusting God. They believe in giving.

Bishop and First Lady White love covering a multitude of sin, meaning praying for and helping people is what the they are about. The first lady promotes all churches. They go to churches to be a blessing, helping in any way they can.

CHAPTER 17

Ms. Janis Jones is a good friend and neighbor. She always has a plan that you can do better, making sure you have taken the time to count the cost of your actions. She is a very kind person.

CHAPTER 18

Stuart Allison is my friend, mentor, husband, and covering for over fifty-four years. He is my go-to person. He always puts our family first. Let go and Let God.

> *Pleasant words are a honeycomb, sweet to the*
> *soul and healing to the bones.* (Proverbs 16:24)

CHAPTER 19

A family gave me a new lease on life.

On August 15, 2015, Chantee needed a babysitter. Someone told her about me. God bless Minister Deidra Clark. I was and still am grateful to have them be a part of our lives. She had twins, Hayden and Hunter, and her niece, Taylor. Ronald is her husband. That was and is a special place in my life. God knows what each and every one of us needs. Being useful and wanted is a part of good life. I thank God for being needed and being able to help someone else. Thank you to the Bingham family.

> *Blessed are the pure in heart: for they shall see God.* (Matthew 5:8)

This story is about a great man, my father's brother. He was my Uncle Thess. He was his brother's keeper. The question was often asked, "Are you your brother's keeper?" I learned as a young girl my Uncle Thess took care of us. My father had an illness. He loved all of us but couldn't provide for us all the time. There were fourteen of us, eight boys and six girls. We were considered poor, but we enjoyed our childhood. Uncle Thess would visit twice a year bringing us clothes, shoes, and coats for Christmas so that we would be prepared for the school year. One Christmas, he made sure he got us toys, clothes, and candy. Then he would talk to us about our grades and schoolwork. Most importantly, he talked to our father about love and kindness. Sometimes he would take me back to his house to help with a party.

Uncle Thess worked for the Williamsburg Inn. He served President and First Lady Nixon. He served the Queen of England and other foreign dignitaries and other presidents. He retired after fifty-one years of service. His wife and children were very good too, and I thank God every day for the love they showed to us as a family. Remember to always do good. Pass it down: "I am my brother's keeper." The answer is yes! Remember only what you do for Christ will last.

The Lord is full of Compassion and Mercy.
(James 5:11)

Sisters of love and joy

All in our seventies! Catherine, 76; Ella, 74; Rosa, 72; Mary, 71

Our youngest in her late sixties, Arneatia, 68

God is still blessing us!

To Christian Faith Publishing,

I, Catherine, owe each person who had a hand in making this book possible. A big thank you and God bless!

ABOUT THE AUTHOR

Catherine Judkins Allison was born in Surry County, Virginia, to John and Ella Judkins. Catherine was the sixth of fourteen children. The author attended Luther P. Jackson Elementary School and graduated from George W. Carver. She later attended the School of Automation for Computers. Catherine went to school for ministry. She works in the church as a Sunday school teacher, serves the women's ministry, and assists the youth ministry. She is often called Go Go Grandma. She was encouraged to write this book to help others who were told they were not going to make it. She has five children, ten grandchildren, and one great-grandchild. She has been married for fifty-four years to the love of her life, Stuart Allison.